The Poetry of

the Mass

Frank
Amato
PORTLAND

Christ's Mass

€ach day tens of thousands of Masses are celebrated throughout the world in scores of different languages. As you read the words in this book meditate on the fact that millions of our fellow human beings will also be worshiping the God who made them with the same meaningful words. Continual Eucharistic worship is being given to God through the Mass as his Son Jesus Christ directed us to do in the bible.

Just twenty centuries ago twelve witnesses (the Apostles whom Christ chose to be his first teachers and ministers) learned the most intimate truths about God which Christ revealed to them: why we were created, who created us, what our creator expects of us and what happens to each of us after we physically die. Then he was crucified on a cross

by those he had created in order to atone for all the sins of the whole human race. Christ as both God and man, showing his unlimited love for us, suffered the ultimate physical act of dying a humiliating, painful death to give us eternal life with him.

On the night before he was crucified and died he did something very special with his closest disciples: he shared his Last Supper with them. Two thousand years later we each can participate as though we were at the Last Supper ourselves—and we can do this every day! At the supper he told them he would shortly offer his body and blood for all people—thus making the ultimate sacrifice. He took simple bread and wine and asked them to eat it, for it was his own body and blood and he commanded them to continue to do what he had done in his memory. *Thus the Eucharist, was given to us directly by Jesus Christ, both God and man.*

The day after Christ instituted the Eucharist he suffered and died on a cross. To the utter amazement of his apostles and other followers, three days later he arose from the dead! Now there was no doubt left in their minds. *Christ indeed was the Son of God.* After seeing the incredible miracle of the risen Christ—their once crucified friend and teacher—his followers were now filled with an enthusiasm that no other event could have kindled. They quickly spread this wonderful news throughout both the Roman and the outside world and the apostles' successors have been doing so ever since, so that in a short twenty centuries Christianity has become the largest world religion, encompassing one third of the world's population.

The bread and wine which we present at Mass is changed into Christ's body and blood (while still keeping the appearance of bread and wine), through the words of the celebrant of the Mass—a priest, who has been ordained by a bishop—and the action of the Holy Spirit. Catholic Christians are encouraged to receive the body and blood of Christ (communion) each time they attend Mass, but only if they are not in a state of serious sin (which requires confession).

The reception of the Eucharist—Christ's body and blood—is an unequalled opportunity to improve our lives and obtain the strength to bear whatever burdens and hardships come our way. Additionally, participation in the Mass gives us the opportunity to pray to God for family members, friends, and world  peace as well as asking God to give us personal strength. Waiting just a few blocks or miles from you is a Catholic Church where Mass is celebrated each day and where you can be a full participant in receiving Christ's body if you but take the invitation.

For nearly 2,000 years Christians have celebrated the Mass and received Christ's body and blood in order to help them in their lives. The Mass is the greatest human experience we can have. The two thousand years of the Mass is the faithful response of the Church to Christ's request in the New Testament: "Do this in memory of me."

From the very beginning Christians celebrated the Eucharistic feast by coming together and breaking bread and sharing the cup as commanded by Christ. As centuries passed and Christianity became the major world religion using a multitude of different languages and various rites in different cultures, the Eucharistic feast (Mass) became more formalized. For the Catholic travelling throughout the world it is a very comforting and inspiring experience to attend Masses celebrated in different languages and in the different rites of the Church, but all with the exact same meaning. Each celebration represents the Church's response to Christ's command: "Do this in memory of me."

Where is the Mass Celebrated?

In the early years when there were few Christians, the Eucharist was celebrated by small groups in people's homes, and in times of persecution it was even celebrated in cemeteries. Once Christianity became legal and the number of Christians grew, churches were built. As Christianity became the majority religious belief in Europe and

persecutions ended, Christ believers built many beautiful churches and cathedrals in God's honor employing many of the finest craftsmen and artists—for after all, the church is where the Lord's Supper is celebrated each day and is a sacred place and center of the community. However, the Mass can be celebrated anywhere when necessary, including homes.

In centuries past beautiful churches built to honor God also had another uplifting effect. Back then the majority population was poor and illiterate. Only a few wealthy

people had beautiful surroundings. But the poor had their beautiful churches with comforting life-like statues and paintings telling the story of creation and Christ's love for them and their families—and providing the wonderful experience of the Mass.

Jesus Christ

Jesus Christ is both true God and true man. Though born of the Virgin Mary, he was truly God's only begotten Son. He lived for about thirty-three years and the last three of these years he taught extensively and gathered a following of twelve Apostles and many other disciples. He was crucified on a cross and three days later rose from the dead—*thus proving that he indeed was God and that what he had taught the Apostles in the previous three years was true.* The Apostles, overwhelmed by the incredible event of Christ's death on the cross and then resurrection three days later, eagerly and authoritatively began teaching his message of love, forgiveness and our eternal happiness with God after death. Their successors (bishops) continue this teaching and all Christians seek to live in accord with Christ's teachings.

XII

INRI

Jesus dies on the Cross

Mary the Mother of God

As the Bible tells us, Christ became flesh in Mary's womb by the action of the Holy Spirit, the third person of the Holy Trinity which is God (the Father, the Son, and the Holy Spirit). Thus Mary is indeed the Mother of God and should be accorded tremendous love, respect and admiration. As the Mother of God she immediately became an example of God's powerful love for us all. Her status as Mother of God helped elevate Western women to equal status with men.

Joseph

Sometimes over-looked by Christians, Mary's older husband Joseph looked after and cared for Jesus throughout his early life. Joseph is considered the ideal model of a loving and understanding husband. In our day his model is much needed.

THE MASS

Introductory Rites

Entrance Song

The Lord fed his people with the finest wheat and honey; their hunger was satisfied.

Greeting

In the name of the Father, and of the Son, and of the Holy Spirit.

Amen.

The grace of our Lord Jesus Christ and the love of God and the fellowship of the Holy Spirit be with you all.

And also with you.

Penitential Rite

*Coming together as God's family,
with confidence let us ask for the Father's forgiveness,
for he is full of gentleness and compassion.*

I confess to almighty God,
and to you, my brothers and sisters,
that I have sinned through my own fault
in my thoughts and in my words,
in what I have done,
and in what I have failed to do;
and I ask blessed Mary, ever virgin,
all the angels and saints,
and you, my brothers and sisters,
to pray for me to the Lord our God.

*May almighty God have mercy on us,
forgive us our sins,
and bring us to everlasting life.*

Amen.

Each day of the year certain Bible readings in the Mass change to reflect the liturgical year and the life of Christ and His teachings. The Mass in this book is for the Solemnity of the Body and Blood of Christ, also know as Corpus Christi Sunday, and is celebrated in late spring of each year.

The words spoken by the priest are in italics and the words spoken by the congregation are in green.

Kyrie

Lord, have mercy.
Lord, have mercy.
Christ, have mercy.
Christ, have mercy.
Lord, have mercy.
Lord, have mercy.

Gloria

lory to God in the highest,
and peace to his people on earth.

Lord God, heavenly King,
almighty God and Father,
we worship you, we give you thanks,
we praise you for your glory.

Lord Jesus Christ, only son of the Father,
Lord God, Lamb of God,
you take away the sin of the world:
have mercy on us;
you are seated at the right hand of the Father:
receive our prayer.

For you alone are the Holy One,
you alone are the Lord,
you alone are the Most High,
Jesus Christ,
with the Holy Spirit,
in the glory of God the Father. Amen.

Let us pray

Lord Jesus Christ,
you gave us the eucharist
as the memorial of your suffering
*   and death.*
May our worship of this sacrament
*   of your body and blood*
help us to experience the salvation
*   you won for us*
and the peace of the kingdom
where you live with the Father and
*   the Holy Spirit,*
one God, for ever and ever.

Amen

Liturgy of the Word

First Reading

Deuteronomy 8:2-3. 14-16

Reader: A reading from the book of Deuteronomy.

Moses said to the people:

"Remember how for forty years now the Lord, your God, has directed all your journeying in the desert, so as to test you by affliction and find out whether or not it was your intention to keep his commandments. He therefore let you be afflicted with hunger, and then fed you with manna, a food unknown to you and your fathers, in order to show you that not by bread alone does man live, but by every word that comes forth from the mouth of the Lord.

"Remember, the Lord, your God, who brought you out of the land of Egypt, that place of slavery; who guided you through the vast and terrible desert with its seraph serpents and scorpions, its parched and waterless ground; who brought forth water for you from the flinty rock and fed you in the desert with manna, a food unknown to your fathers."

Reader: The word of the Lord.

Thanks be to God.

Responsorial Psalm

Psalm 147: 12-13, 14-15, 19-20

Cantor: Praise the Lord, Jerusalem.

Praise the Lord, Jerusalem.

> *Glorify the Lord, O Jerusalem;*
> *praise your god, O Zion.*
> *For he has strengthened the bars of your gates;*
> *he has blessed your children within you.*

Praise the Lord, Jerusalem.

> *He has granted peace in your borders;*
> *with the best of wheat he fills you.*
> *He sends forth his command to the earth;*
> *swiftly runs his word!*

Praise the Lord, Jerusalem.

> *He has proclaimed his word to Jacob,*
> *his statutes and his ordinances to Israel.*
> *He has not done thus for any other nation;*
> *his ordinances he has not made known to them.*
> *Alleluia.*

Praise the Lord, Jerusalem.

Second Reading

1 Corinthians 10: 16-17

Reader: A reading from the first letter of Paul to the Corinthians.

Is not the cup of blessing we bless a sharing in the blood of Christ? And is not the bread we break a sharing in the body of Christ? Because the loaf of bread is one, we, many though we are, are one body for we all partake of the one loaf.

Reader: The word of the Lord.

Thanks be to God.

Alleluia

Alleluia, alleluia

Cantor: I am the living bread from heaven, says the Lord; if anyone eats this bread he will live for ever.

Alleluia, alleluia

Gospel

John 6: 51-58

Deacon or Priest
The Lord be with you.

And also with you.

Deacon or Priest
A reading from the holy gospel according to John.

Glory to you, Lord.

Deacon or Priest
Jesus said to the crowds of Jews:

"I myself am the living bread come down from heaven. If anyone eats this bread he shall live for ever; the bread I will give is my flesh, for the life of the world."

At this the Jews quarreled among themselves, saying, "How can he give us his flesh to eat?" Thereupon Jesus said to them:

"Let me solemnly assure you, if you do not eat the flesh of the Son of Man and drink his blood, you have no life in you. He who feeds on my flesh and drinks my blood has life eternal, and I will raise him up on the last day. For my flesh is real food and my blood real drink. The man who feeds on my flesh and drinks my blood remains in me, and I in him. Just as the Father who has life sent me and I have life because of the Father, so the man who feeds on me will have life because of me. This is the bread that came down from heaven. Unlike your ancestors who ate and died nonetheless, the man who feeds on this bread shall live forever."

The gospel of the Lord.

Praise to you, Lord Jesus Christ.

Homily

We believe in one God,
the Father, the Almighty,
maker of heaven and earth,
of all that is seen and unseen.

We believe in one Lord, Jesus Christ,
the only Son of God,
eternally begotten of the Father,
God from God, Light from Light,
true God from true God,
begotten, not made, one in Being with the Father.
Through him all things were made.
For us men and for our salvation
he came down from heaven:
by the power of the Holy Spirit
he was born of the Virgin Mary, and became man.

For our sake he was crucified under Pontius Pilate;
he suffered, died, and was buried.
On the third day he rose again
in fulfillment of the Scriptures;
he ascended into heaven
and is seated at the right hand of the Father.
He will come again in glory to judge the living and the dead,
and his kingdom will have no end.

We believe in the Holy Spirit, the Lord, the giver of life,
who proceeds from the Father and the Son.
With the Father and the Son he is worshiped and glorified.
He has spoken through the Prophets.
We believe in one holy catholic and apostolic Church.
We acknowledge one baptism for the forgiveness of sins.
We look for the resurrection of the dead,
and the life of the world to come. Amen.

General Intercessions

Lord, hear our prayer.

Liturgy of the Eucharist

Presentation of the Gifts

Blessed are you, Lord, God of all creation.
Through your goodness we have this bread to offer,
which earth has given and human hands have made.
It will become for us the bread of life.

Blessed be God for ever.

Blessed are you, Lord, God of all creation.
Through your goodness we have this wine to offer,
fruit of the vine and work of human hands.
It will become our spiritual drink.

Blessed be God for ever.

Prayer Over the Gifts

Pray, brethren, that our sacrifice may be acceptable to
God, the almighty Father.

May the Lord accept the sacrifice at your hands
for the praise and glory of his name,
for our good, and the good of all his Church.

Lord, may the bread and cup we offer
bring your Church the unity and peace they signify.
We ask this in the name of Jesus the Lord.

Amen.

Eucharistic Prayer
Preface

The Lord be with you.
And also with you.
Lift up your hearts.
We lift them up to the Lord.
Let us give thanks to the Lord our God.
It is right to give him thanks and praise.

Father, all-powerful and ever-living God,
we do well always and everywhere to give you thanks
through Jesus Christ our Lord.

He is the true and eternal priest
who established this unending sacrifice.
He offered himself as a victim for our deliverance
and taught us to make this offering in his memory.
As we eat his body which he gave for us,
we grow in strength.
As we drink his blood which he poured out for us,
we are washed clean.

Now, with angels and archangels,
and the whole company of heaven,
we sing the unending hymn of your praise:

Sanctus

Holy, holy, holy Lord, God of power and might,
heaven and earth are full of your glory.
　　Hosanna in the highest.
Blessed is he who comes in the name of the Lord.
　　Hosanna in the highest.

 e come to you, Father,
with praise and thanksgiving,
through Jesus Christ your Son.

Through him we ask you to accept and bless
these gifts we offer you in sacrifice.

We offer them for your holy catholic Church,
watch over it, Lord, and guide it;
grant it peace and unity throughout the world.
We offer them for John Paul our Pope,
for our N. (the local bishop),
and for all who hold and teach the catholic faith
that comes to us from the apostles.

Remember, Lord, your people,
especially those for whom we now pray.
Remember all of us gathered here before you.
You know how firmly we believe in you
and dedicate ourselves to you.
We offer you this sacrifice of praise
for ourselves and those who are dear to us.
We pray to you, our living and true God,
for our well-being and redemption.

In union with the whole Church
we honor Mary,
the ever-virgin mother of Jesus Christ our Lord and God.
We honor Joseph, her husband,
the apostles and martyrs
Peter and Paul, Andrew,
and all the saints.
May their merits and prayers
gain us your constant help and protection.

(Through Christ our Lord. Amen.)

Father accept this offering
for your whole family.
Grant us your peace in this life,
save us from final damnation,
and count us among those you have chosen.

(Through Christ our Lord. Amen.)

Bless and approve our offering;
make it acceptable to you,
an offering in spirit and in truth.
Let it become for us
the body and blood of Jesus Christ,
your only Son, our Lord.

The day before he suffered
he took bread in his sacred hands
and looking up to heaven,
to you, his almighty Father,
he gave you thanks and praise.
He broke the bread,
gave it to his disciples, and said:

> Take this, all of you and eat it:
> this is my body which will be given up for you.

"That the Eucharist conveyed to the believer the Body and Blood of Christ was universally accepted from the first, and language was very commonly used which referred to the Eucharistic elements as themselves the Body and Blood."
— *The Oxford Dictionary of the Christian Church*

When supper was ended,
he took the cup.
Again he gave you thanks and praise,
gave the cup to his disciples, and said:

> **Take this, all of you, and drink from it:**
> **this is the cup of my blood,**
> **the blood of the new and everlasting covenant.**
> **It will be shed for you and for all**
> **so that sins may be forgiven.**
> **Do this in memory of me.**

Memorial Acclamation

Let us proclaim the mystery of faith:

Dying you destroyed our death;
rising you restored our life.
Lord Jesus, come in glory.

-or-

When we eat this bread and drink this cup,
we proclaim your death, Lord Jesus,
until you come in glory.

-or-

Lord, by your cross and resurrection
you have set us free.
You are the Savior of the world.

Father, we celebrate the memory of Christ, your Son.
We, your people and your ministers,
recall his passion,
his resurrection from the dead,
and his ascension into glory;
and from the many gifts you have given us
we offer to you, God of glory and majesty,
this holy and perfect sacrifice:
the bread of life and the cup of eternal salvation.

Look with favor on these offerings
and accept them as once you accepted
the gifts of your servant Abel,
the sacrifice of Abraham, our father in faith,
and the bread and wine offered by your priest Melchisedech.

Almighty God,
we pray that your angel may take this sacrifice
to your altar in heaven.
Then, as we receive from this altar
the sacred body and blood of your Son,
let us be filled with every grace and blessing.

(Through Christ our Lord. Amen.)

Remember, Lord, those who have died
and have gone before us marked with the sign of faith,
especially those for whom we now pray.
May these, and all who sleep in Christ,
find in your presence
light, happiness, and peace.

(Through Christ our Lord. Amen.)

For ourselves, too, we ask
some share in the fellowship of your apostles and martyrs,
with John the Baptist, Stephen, Matthias, Barnabas,
    Ignatius, Alexander, Marcellinus, Peter,
    Felicity, Perpetua, Agatha, Lucy,
    Agnes, Cecilia, Anastasia
and all the saints.
Though we are sinners,
we trust in your mercy and love.
Do not consider what we truly deserve,
but grant us your forgiveness.

Through Christ our Lord.

Through him you give us all these gifts.
You fill them with life and goodness,
you bless them and make them holy.

Through him,
with him,
in him,
in the unity of the Holy Spirit,
all glory and honor is yours,
almighty Father,
for ever and ever.

Amen.

S. FRANCISCO JAVIER

Communion Rite

The Lord's Prayer

Let us pray with confidence to the Father in the words our Savior gave us.

Our Father,
who art in heaven,
hallowed be thy name;
thy kingdom come;
thy will be done,
on earth as it is in heaven.
Give us this day our daily bread;
and forgive us our trespasses
as we forgive those who trespass against us;
and lead us not into temptation,
but deliver us from evil.

Deliver us, Lord, from every evil,
and grant us peace in our day.
In your mercy keep us free from sin
and protect us from all anxiety
as we wait in joyful hope
for the coming of our Savior, Jesus Christ.

For the kingdom,
the power and the glory are yours,
now and forever.

Sign of Peace

Lord Jesus Christ, you said to your apostles:
I leave you peace, my peace I give you.
Look not on our sins, but on the faith of your Church,
and grant us the peace and unity of your kingdom
where you live for ever and ever.

Amen.

The peace of the Lord be with you always.

And also with you.

Let us offer each other the sign of peace.

Breaking of the Bread

Lamb of God, you take away the sins of the world:
   have mercy on us.
Lamb of God, you take away the sins of the world:
   have mercy on us.
Lamb of God, you take away the sins of the world:
   grant us peace.

May this mingling of the body and blood of our Lord Jesus Christ
bring eternal life to us who receive it.

Lord Jesus Christ, Son of the living God, by the will of the Father and the work of the Holy Spirit your death brought life to the world. By your holy body and blood free me from all my sins, and from every evil. Keep me faithful to your teaching, and never let me be parted from you.

-or-

Lord Jesus Christ, with faith in your love and mercy I eat your body and drink your blood. Let it not bring me condemnation, but health in my mind and body.

Communion

*This is the Lamb of God
who takes away the sins of the world.
Happy are those who are called to his supper.*

Lord, I am not worthy to receive you, but only say the word and I shall be healed.

Communion Song

Whoever eats my flesh and drinks my blood will live in me and I in him, says the Lord.

(John 6:57)

Lord Jesus Christ,
you give us your body and blood in the eucharist
as a sign that even now we share your life.
May we come to possess it completely in the kingdom
where you live for ever and ever.

Amen.

Concluding Rite

Blessing

The Lord be with you.

And also with you.

May almighty God bless you, the Father, and the Son,
and the Holy Spirit.

Amen.

Dismissal

Go in peace to love and serve the Lord.

Thanks be to God.

Prayers after Mass

Anima Christi

Soul of Christ, sanctify me;
Body of Christ, save me;
Blood of Christ, inebriate me;
Water from the side of Christ, wash me;
Passion of Christ, strengthen me;
O good Jesus, hear me;
Within your wounds hide me;
Separated from you, let me never be;
From the evil one protect me;
At the hour of my death, call me;
And close to you bid me;
That with your saints, I may be,
praising you for ever and ever.
Amen

Prayer Before The Crucifix

Behold O kind and gentle Jesus, I kneel before you and pray that you would impress upon my heart the virtues of faith, hope and charity, with true repentance for my sins and a firm purpose of amendment. At the same time, with sorrow I meditate on your five precious wounds, having in mind the words which David spoke in prophecy: "They have pierced my hands and my feet. I can count all my bones." (Ps 22)